AZOREAN CUISINE

AZOREAN CUISINE

AUTHOR **ZITA LIMA**

PROLOGUE **VASCO PEREIRA DA COSTA**

EVEREST EDITORA

AZOREAN CUISINE

An Introduction

In an archipelago of nine islands between Europe and America, land and sea, naturally, condition its civilisational manifestations – and the gastronomy, sublime and perfect chemical combination, confers memory, wisdom and impetus of genius, consecrated in the marks of time.

The elements provide us all that is good. And Azoreans transform all that nature provides into a delicacy.

Memories of spice-fragrant vessels were associated to their European condition and unheard of products from all corners of the world were adopted.

Thus, by paying close attention to it, one discovers intensified flavours, delicate aromas, masterly colours, subtle transformations – in the manner and in an era of affirming an identity and of testifying to the intimacy with the roundness of the world.

VASCO PEREIRA DA COSTA
(AUTHOR)

INTRODUCTION

The Azores archipelago is formed by 9 islands. It is said that its name will have originated due to the great number of kites to be found there, which were mistaken then with into a delicacy *açores*. The legend also goes that the archipelago is nothing but what was left of Atlantida, the great legendary continent situated in the Atlantic thousands of years ago.

It is an archipelago of volcanic origin, shaken throughout the years, by various tremors of the most varied levels, the last of which – in Faial, in 1998, and in Terceira, in 1980 – reached earthquake proportions, the effects of which are still visible and remain in the memory of many Azoreans.

As previously mentioned, there are nine islands: Santa Maria, São Miguel, Terceira, Graciosa, São Jorge, Pico, Faial, Flores and Corvo. The largest is São Miguel with a maximum length of 62km and its largest width of 16km, and with a population of about 131,510 inhabitants.

The smallest, Corvo, stretches along a length of about 5,5km and at a width of 2km. Its population consists of around 418 inhabitants. By way of curiosity, I might add that the highest point of Portugal is in the Azores, in the second largest island: the mountain of Pico, with an altitude of 2, 350metres.

All the islands are of a surprising beauty, each one with its landscapes, lagoons, mountains, flora and even celebrations with their own specific characteristics. Discovered by an increasing number of tourists, these are unanimous in declaring them "unique" and prove enchanted by being able to visit them.

A frank, open, cheerful, hard-working and artistic people, as proven by their handicrafts that go from beautiful embroidery, to lovely spun bedspreads, to artistic pieces made of fig tree kernel or fish scales, to the exquisite engravings in whale bone and teeth, to the wicker work, ceramics and so many others which well deserve to be seen, appreciated and promoted.

"The Azorean people live in contact with the world, as it was born, created and procreated into a family in full Atlantic, an ocean that does not constitute isolation but rather an invitation to knowledge of other lands – and we should stress all the American Republics as countries that are known directly or through dialogues with the returnees *"torna viagem"* of which any family rarely lacks a representative. Thus its spirit is not closed to new things [...] In fact, the Azorean producer rarely knows what he has applied in terms of seeds. These emerge from the granary or from the warehouse without being counted and are countlessly thrown on the soil." (Bulletin nº 8 of the Cereal Regulatory Commission of the Archipelago of the Azores).

GASTRONOMY AND TRADITION

Who would ever say that what was so many times asked of me – to put to paper some of the recipes that I collected in various islands – would ever come true...

As one might guess, it did not prove to be an easy task and for many reasons: there are 9 islands, each one with its specialities and traditions, but at the same time, with recipes which, after having been better savoured, do vary, although at first glance they maybe seem the same and sometimes, even with the same name, be it in the main ingredient, be it in the simple exchange a parsley sprig for a sprig of mint, be it because in this one the meat is cured in salt, and in that one it is seasoned à la minute, or because one has to be made with red wine (vinho de cheiro), and another with white wine...and so on. For example, the name of a dessert may be the same; however, the history of that dessert, that one is indeed different.

In fact, even with the names of villages or parishes that happens. Let us see now: Lages das Flores, Lages do Pico and in Terceira, a Lages parish. Likewise in Flores, Santa Cruz is the town but in Graciosa, Santa Cruz is the name given to the main town of the island. And many other repetitions are to be found such as Ponta Delgada, Santa Bárbara, Santo Amaro, Candelária, Ribeirinha, Feteira, etc.

Thus to choose the thirty recipes I was asked for, from many others, was no easy task. This because besides the regional gastronomy in its entirety being rich, be it in taste, be it in condiments, it is impossible to state with all certainty: this is typical of Pico, of Faial or of any other island. Clearly, even on the same island, from parish to parish there are different ways of cooking. An ingredient that is used in one and in another it is said that "Here it is not used."

I am specifically referring to the soups of the

Holy Ghost (*Espírito Santo*). An opportunity was already afforded me of tasting them, in more than one island. And even in Terceira, where I live, in different parishes I have never tried two with a similar taste.

I regret not having included in this book the recipe of the Soups of the Holy Ghost (*Sopas do Espírito Santo*), but in order for this soup to be more than just a simple meat soup, there is a whole series of factors and rituals that, jointly, are able to turn a meat soup into the delicacy that makes us have second, and even third, helpings. It starts with the preparation of the slaughtered animal destined at the offset to the Divine Holy Ghost. Afterwards, it is the blessing of the meats that, after being cut, are placed on long benches, decorated with sprigs with the Crown of the Holy Ghost among them. The making of this appetising repast is also characteristic and unique.

On the day that follows the killing of the animal, at the crack of dawn, one finds men and women preparing the enormous iron pans, which are set out under the open sky, above special tripods, on incandescent firewood trunks. There, we see some preparing the meats and the chickens, others cleaning and cutting the cabbages or "*couves de bola*", others still peeling potatoes, alas, to place all that is necessary at hand by the "Master of the Service" ("*Mestre de Função*"): boiling water, sprinkling seasoning, from the salt to the peppers, to the meats, to the lard, to the butter and to such condiments or ingredients as each Master ("*Mestre*") may deem to know as a personal secret.

In the meantime, in another area, women get busy with the bread, especially baked for the "Soups" ("*Sopas*"), which also has its ritual, in the slicing and placing in white bowls, normally loaned by the pantry of the Empire of each parish.

In the morning, some rump or *alcatras de "batacozes"* (bones) have also been made, the gravy or *molha* of which is destined to aromatise the respective bread soups, on the slices of which a sprig of mint is placed. As soon as the meats are cooked, the broth is strained and poured over the bread to soak it.

On the whitest of tablecloths are placed bowls, filled with the soups and covered with a plate, smothered with rugs to preserve the heat. Before being taken to the tables, set with large planks and trestle normally out in the open air, the soups are blessed by the Priest who celebrated the Service Mass (*Missa da Função*).

Next, one feels the enraptured look with which each one gets served! If you like the "Soups" ("*Sopas*") dryer, place the ladle on the top; if you like them soaking, go to the bottom, once, twice or, who knows, one more time still. It's just that the 2Soups of the Holy Ghost" ("*Sopas do Espírito Santo*") are really good! And with the blessing of the Holy Ghost.

Another very typical festivity, and which greatly attracts the curious, is the Procession of the *rosquilhas* ("*Procissão das Rosquilhas*") (rings of sweet bread, a kind of *massa sovada*), on the island of Pico. I was given the opportunity to witness this procession in Criação Velha, a parish near Vila da Madalena. In quite a long garden, men and women with large wicker baskets decorated with lacy tablecloths and filled with a vast quantity of *rosquilhas, loirinhas, tostadas*, decorated with carnations and white lilies descend on each side. Next, to see who has the best-decorated basket! The "quatrain" ("*quadras*"), four young girls dressed in white, holding four poles follows in the centre. In the first quatrain follows the banner, in the second, the Crown of the Holy Ghost (*Coroa do Espírito Santo*) and, in the third, finally comes the Priest. At the end of the procession, the baskets are placed on wooden benches, which are to be found in this garden; next, these are blessed by the Priest, while the Philharmonic plays the hymn to the Holy Ghost. After this ceremony, the *rosquilhas* are placed in trucks lined with white sheets and distributed by all those present at this festivity.

By way of curiosity, I can say that in the Tuesday procession of the year 2002 'only' 8,000 *rosquilhas* were made.

In the northern part of the island of Pico cakes are distributed the day before, of a harder dough than those made on the island of São Jorge but also exhibiting the marks of the 'large keys' ('chavões'), with symbols of the Holy Ghost, on the dough.

I would also like to mention, although very much in passing, the sugar-paste or *alfenim*, a sweet based on sugar and water, which, after reaching a certain point, is 'pulled' and 'folded' until one is able to mould it and make figurines, edible, of course, ranging from animals, *rosquilhas*, legs, arms, etc, which, in the latter examples, serve as promise offerings to the Holy Ghost and which are later auctioned in favour of the Empire. There would be a lot more to write about traditions in a place where gastronomy is ever-present.

FOODS FROM THE LAND AND THE SEA
Meats

In the Azores bovine meat of excellent quality is produced, predominantly on the islands of São Miguel, Terceira and Pico. This quality partly comes from the feeding component of the animals, which consists above all of pasture of very good quality, which is grown in the region throughout the whole year, given the mild climacteric conditions that are to be found there.

The production of pork meat also has great potential, not only for its quality but also for being almost naturally protected from the great epidemics that are found in the continents, namely the African swine plague, among others. Chickens, turkeys, ducks and rabbits are also raised on rations, corn and greens. There is also some game, especially rabbits.

Fish, Seafood and Molluscs

With an economic zone ("ZEE") of 1 million square metres, due to the dispersion of the 9 islands, combined with the wealth of it fishing banks, the region presents a great variety, of great quality, of the piscicultural species. Among them are the *tunídeos* that are handled in great quantities by industrial units located in the region.

I will mention some of the many fish pulled out of the seas of the Azores: squirrelfish, *boca negra*, teleost fish, *cântaro*, saurel, mackerel, grouper, *encharéu*, sword-fish (*espadarte*), sea-bream (*goraz, pargo*), marracho; sword-fish (*espada*), moray, horse-mackerel, rock-fish, conger or sea-eel, saw-fish, *salema* and pigfish, and many, many more. With regards to the seafood, the most typical in the region is the limpet ('lapa'), served in various ways but which, even if merely grilled, is always a delicious dish.

Also very well-known is the *cavaco*, a shellfish that is from the lobster family, spider-crab, crab and still *búzios*.

As far as molluscs are concerned, the most appreciated is the octopus followed by the squid, also abundant in the seas of the Azores.

I cannot fail to speak of barnacles or 'cracas', a much appreciated shellfish, which has the characteristic of being caught or gathered underwater, by the force of a chisel and hammer as the receptacle – or 'point' ('bico'), as is usually said – into which it is inserted, is normally formed on the actual rock. Its cooking warrants care, as its points have to be placed into the pot facing up, so that the liquid inside them, which has a very unique taste, not at all comparable to other shellfish, is not lost. To be eaten, they have to be removed from the 'points' ('bicos') with the aid of a nail with a bent end.

OTHER PRODUCTS
The Olive

In the Azores there are some olive trees, with greater incidence in Terceira, in Porto Martim, and some in Pico, at Criação Velha. According to a report by a producer from Porto Martim, a

Mister João Areias, I found out how the olive harvest and preparation in this region is done.

The olive is picked by hand, placed into a bag that is tied to the waist and, when one estimates that there are about 4-5 kg in it, the olives are thrown into wicker baskets with two handles. One sole man is sufficient to pick more or less 40 kg of olives in one day.

The olives next go into a wooden mash-tub, with water, that is changed daily for 10 days. After this period, follows the salt curing.

For a mash-tub of 200 litres, which may take 150kg of olives, 15kg of salt will be needed. And that was all that was done then. Currently, this producer still prepares the olives in the same way in the mash-tubs, with the water, and for 10 days, but places them next, in layers, alternating garlic, bay leaf and oreganum. He covers them with a sackcloth bag which is tied around the mash-tub, and only then does he empty out the curing salt, covering it straight after.

After 3 months it is ready to be served. It was mentioned to me, however, that there are those who pick out some of the more developed ones, make 3 cuts into each olive, passing them through 3 boiling waters, changing them while lukewarm, draining and preparing them afterwards as per the previous method. In this case, they can be eaten 24 hours later.

Tea

"Widely divulged, especially in the East, it is unknown how the cultivation of tea began to be practised in the Azores.

The first news we know of about that dates back to 1801, attesting to the fact that such cultivation was done on the island of Terceira, already at the end of the 18th century. However, it was only in the middle of the 19th century that the cultivation of tea was to show great increment in the Azores, particularly on the island of São Miguel." (Information from Bulletin nº 15 of the Cereals Commission of the Archipelago of the Azores).

In São Miguel, I went to visit the *Gorreana* tea cultivation. I will present here, in a succinct manner, the facts and techniques, from that visit, that lead to the preparation of the tea, as they were transmitted to me by the proprietor, Engineer Hermano Atayde Mota. On 32 hectares, the plants grow, blossom, are picked and the plantations are renewed.

The first plants came from China, via Macau, in 1874. Their leaves, however, failed to reach more than 1 to 2 cm in size. Thus, in 1949, various seeds were imported from India, the leaves of which, being bigger, allowed for a more profitable commercialisation.

The renewal of the plant is spontaneously done and this way, the two qualities were naturally combined. Each plant lasts, technically, 90 years, and the leaves, to reach the required size, need about 6 years.

The picking begins in April and lasts until September. Only the first 3 leaves of each plant give rise to tea. The offshoots, in the meantime, continue growing and appearing every 12-13 days, so that once again, the first 3 leaves of each plant are picked.

In 1960, the first harvest machines were introduced and, until 1971, this was simultaneously done by machine and by hand. Currently, by using a special pruning that enables the plants to be in a good condition to receive the machine, the whole harvest is done mechanically.

There are some differences in the preparation of the leaves of black or green tea. The difference is the time that the leaves will spend drying out, the passage through the machine that rolls them and later crinkles them up, and the pressing. For black tea, after the whole preparation beforehand, the leaves are spread out on trays and laid out in the open air to oxidise, for more or less 3 hours. It is only afterwards that they are placed to dry in a suitable hothouse and are separated by screens and placed in a wind sieve so as to obtain the various qualities: Orange Peckoe, Peckoe, Broken leaf and the *Moinhas*.

For green tea, the sap is let out warming up the leaves with water vapour; they are to remain in the roller only 4-5 minutes, passing afterwards onto the dryer (hothouse) to remove part of the humidity.

Later, the leaves will be boxed and covered by a canvas to avoid contact with the air. There, they will cool for 24 hours. Finally, they will be rolled again and definitively dried.

Speaking of tea, it pleases me to leave the recipe for a refreshing drink made with green tea. Add 1 sprig of mint and lemon slices to the green tea, which is then placed in the fridge. By way of curiosity, I will say that in some houses, in the olden days, this refreshment was served with fried mackerels.

FURNAS OF SÃO MIGUEL

As previously mentioned, all the islands have peculiarities worthy of being appreciated and, in this context, I could not but speak of the caldera region, in the parish of Furnas.

It is an unmatched place which is as beautiful as it is frightening. Vapours emerge from the ground, from mouths of various sizes; the water boils piping hot, the taps pour lukewarm or hot water, all of this surrounding one with a strong sulphur odour. Seeing is believing.

From all of that, benefits may be gained: in the boiling water, corn cobs are introduced placed in canvas bags and there, they are cooked and are then appreciated. On the ground, holes are made with a weeding-hoe where the much appreciated *cozido das furnas* is made. On a table-cloth (which was only used for that purpose), cabbage leaves are spread out in a circumference and on that meats, of pork, beef, chicken, *chouriço*, and *toucinho* and a little bag in which were placed a blood sausage (*morcela*) (so that it

would not come apart and spread out), sweet and normal potatoes, and even carrots, sliced vertically down the middle. Cabbage leaves were placed once again. Of course, the meats had to be previously seasoned with salt.

The tablecloth was then folded over the last leaves, and it would all be wrapped up again in another cloth and next, placed in a well-tied bag of sackcloth, which would be introduced into that hole and which would be covered with the same soil. At the end of 4 to 4 and a half hours the *cozido* was ready. It was then dug out and served. I should tell you that the taste of that *cozido* was comparable to no other. You may have noticed that I have been using verbs in the past. It is just that nowadays *cozido* is rarely made the way I described it. It was decided that, in a certain area, the holes were likewise made in the soil, but covered with a layer of cement.

The *cozido* is made is made nowadays in an aluminium pan, using the same ingredients I have mentioned, but placed in layers. It is covered with an aluminium lid, that is well-tied up from handle to handle with rope, placed in a bag and introduced into the hole in the ground and covered with a lid, also made of cement. There, the cooking time is longer, from 5 to 6 hours.

'Codfish with everything' ('*Bacalhau com todos*') is also cooked in the same way, also using the *chouriço*, bean stew, and sweet cakes (made of chocolate, honey, orange and others), as well as sweet rice (*arroz doce*) and even preserves.

SOME CULTIVATIONS

Among the some of the Azorean cultivations are those of yams, bananas, granadillas, mandarins, guava trees, Brazilian guava, besides that of the pineapple, apple tree, pear tree, prune tree, peach tree, fig tree, orange tree, lemon tree and the grapevine.

But let us speak of the first six:

"There is no Azorean who does not know one of the *ex-libris* of the Azores, the yam. It is a common accompaniment to traditional dishes of Azorean cuisine in almost the whole archipelago. A plant with extraordinary capacities of adaptation to the climacteric conditions of the region, it grows in the most varied types of soil and is very resistant to sickness and inclemency [...]. The cultivation of the yam is done a little all over the island of São Miguel, but the only place where the irrigation is cultivated is in the parish of Furnas [...]. (Extract taken from Information Bulletin of the DRDA – n° 3 of 7/8 1999).

"The introduction of the banana tree in the Azores goes back some centuries ago, when the archipelago constituted a port of call on the return trip to Europe. Firstly, it was part of botanical collections, in the gardens of well-off aristocrats and only more recently, as an intensive cultivation [...]

However, in the last 25-30 years, the cultivation of the banana tree in the region has grown to be target of a greater interest on the part of agriculturalists, as a result of the apparent lack of alternatives in the horticulture and fruit-growing sector [...]. The cultivation of the banana is traditionally destined for local consumption [...] As far as the banana harvest season is concerned, it is practically done throughout the whole year. However, the summer season is the one of greatest production and quality [...]". (*idem*)

"Denomination of origin – Granadilla of São Miguel. The Jesuits, upon finding the granadilla flower, envisaged a symbolic reconstitution of the Passion of Christ: the combination of five sepals and of the five petals would represent the ten Apostles present at the crucifixion, the fringe of *violaceae* would be the crown of thorns, the five anthers would be the wounds and the three macula would be the nails [...]

On the island of São Miguel, the variety – Purple Granadilla – was introduced in the 17th century by the emigrants who brought it as an ornament. It was only at the beginning of the 20th century that the fruit was used to make liqueurs [...] the fruit is a berry of 4 to 5cm in diameter, of purple colouring when ripe, very juicy, of sour taste, but quite pleasant [...]" (*ibidem*)

"The mandarin tree is a tree of greater development than the common tangerine tree [...] when the leaf is rubbed between one's fingers, it has a smell that simultaneously reminds one of that of a tangerine and of a sour orange [...] in actual fact, the mandarin has already acquired the rights to Azorean naturalisation and it is the dessert that is preferred by all of us, during these months of Autumn, while neither the perfumed and the tale-bearing tangerines nor the sweet oranges of the land, that provided so much fame and money in yonder years to the Azores, arrive.
Without speaking, as will be seen, of the pineapple, the king of fruits, which in this hour of crisis, has unfortunately become accessible to the most common of mortals [...]" (Bulletin n° 7 of the Cereal Regulatory Commission of the Archipelago of the Azores).

"[...] The guava tree – this species, like others of the same type, furthermore also known by the generic name of guava, the origin of which is Central America, is found spontaneously from Mexico to the south of Brazil [...] In the Azores, two varieties of the *P. Guayauava* appear: one, of white pulp and the other, of rosy pulp, the second one being considered the best for consumption [...]
It is extremely rich in vitamin C, and in such a way that the orange, until recently considered the richest fruit in this vitamin, is outdone 4 to 10 times by the guava [...] and which gives them the necessary balance to allow for the transformation of the fruits into a paste or jelly of firm

consistency and of good preservation (the *goiaba-da*), thanks furthermore to the OH, in actual values..." (*idem*)

"The Brazilian guava or *araca*, known in the Azores as the *aracaleiro*, is a plant with the same origin of the guava tree and with affinities with the latter already by the characteristics of the fruit, already by the demands of the plant [...] the fruit is small, rounded, with dimensions close to that of the cherry. They are of yellow, red or purple skin and of whitish pulp with hard seeds. In the Azores, the plants of yellow fruits – "white guava", red and purple, these being smaller and astringent – are cultivated [...] In the Azores, the "white guava" bears fruit from September to November and the "red" from October to December, both with a certain regularity [...] The wood can be used in small naval construction and in luxury woodwork [...]" (*ibidem*)

TWO CITRINES IN THE AZOREAN FOLK POETRY

"[...] The orange, like the orange tree, has many and interesting traditions in the lands of the Azores. The antiquity of its cultivation on these islands is well known, as is its history and its economic importance [...]"
With regards to the feelings it may often happen that the best orange – that of air – may be where least expected. As one singer from São Miguel would say to another:

> Don't hope to vie
> With me, uncle John
> As I am fruit of the air
> And you, orange of the ground.

It is still destiny that reigns – as is stated in this quatrain collected in Lagoa –when one states that "the little titbit is kept for the one destined to eat it".

> I have a sweet orange
> At the bottom of my trunk
> To give to my love,
> God willing it be you.
> [...]"

(Bulletin nº 17 of the Cereal Regulatory Commission of the Archipelago of the Azores)

"The lemon tree, [...] with its fruits, for truthfully, there is no one among the people who does not emotional when facing this ruffled tree with thorns but still gracious with its foliage, enchanting for its perfume, suggestive by the fruits hanging from its branches.
Like the golden fruit of the orange tree, the lemon is frequently found not only in folk medicine but also in the actual songs [...]. An acid fruit, like no other citrine, the lemon is, however, recommended for certain debilitating states, is good for the blood and reduces the appetite. Here is a song from São Jorge proclaiming that:

> The lemon is a sour fruit
> That is brought in one's hand for honour;
> I wish I were the lemon
> That removed your appetite.

And the comparison between a lemon and love remains fair, in the poetic images of the Azorean people. This time, it is close to the fruit that the anonymous poet of São Jorge finds the term of comparison for his crying, sad soul:

> The green lemon, picked
> Its stem remains crying;
> Thus are my loves
> When they pass by me
> [...] (*idem*)

BROTH of TURNIPS FROM THE LAND (SANTA MARIA)

This type of turnip, of reduced dimension and of dark colour, only exists in some of the areas in Santa Maria, especially in scarcely productive fields, leaving the attempts of cultivation in more fertile lands outside the island to insuccess. Throughout the years, the Broth of Turnips has constituted one of the typical culinary specialities of the island of Santa Maria.

Time of Consumption FROM SPRING ONWARDS   Recommended for DINNER
Recipe for 6 PEOPLE   Preparation Time 2 HOURS   Level of Difficulty EASY
Recommended Wine REGIONAL, PREFERABLY RED

INGREDIENTS
- 500 g turnips from the land
- 500 g pork meat, from the leg, with bone
- 250 g toucinho entremeado
- 250 g chouriço
- 2 sweet potatoes
- home baked bread
- salt, to taste

1 The turnips are scraped and sliced vertically into slivers. They are scalded in boiling water, which is then discarded.

2 In a second water, they are to boil a little; likewise, the water where they boiled, always without salt, is also discarded.

3 They are washed one more time in hot water and are returned to the heat this time with the meat and *toucinho* (which should be salted the day before), the *chouriço* and the potatoes.

4 Thick slices of home baked bread soaked in the broth are laid on a serving platter.

5 The meat, the *chouriço*, the *toucinho*, the potatoes and the turnips are placed on another serving platter.

TIPS AND TRICKS
- The bread slices may be soaked more or less heavily in the meat broth, according to taste.

SOUR SOUP

There are those who say that this soup was usually made in Faial, but that Terceira adopted it, adding the pumpkin. Thus its exact origin cannot de defined. This soup has a very special taste due to the spices it takes.

Time of Consumption ALL YEAR ROUND   Recommended for LUNCH OR DINNER
Recipe for 8 PEOPLE   Preparation Time ABOUT 2 HOURS   Level of Difficulty AVERAGE
Recommended Wine REGIONAL WINE OF QUALITY

INGREDIENTS
- 1/2 kg. kidney beans
- 1 onion
- 3 leeks
- 2 tablespoons olive oil
- 1/2 kg. pumpkin, already cleaned
- 2 sweet potatoes
- 2 normal potatoes, from the land
- 1 teaspoon cinnamon
- 1 tablespoon sugar
- 2 tablespoons vinegar
- 1/2 coffee spoon of powdered cumin
- salt, to taste

1 Sauté the onion, the leeks and the olive oil. To this sautéed mixture, add the beans, presoaked the day before, and let it boil.

2 Sieve everything and add the spices – cinnamon, sugar, vinegar, salt and cumin – to the purée. Boil to bring out the flavour of the spices.

3 Add the potatoes and the pumpkin, cut into little cubes.

4 Let it boil and taste to check for seasoning.

TIPS AND TRICKS
- Be careful when checking for seasoning as it is important to be able to identify the taste of each spice, without there being a predominance of any one in particular.

FISH BROTH
FROM PICO

This recipe is an example of those broths that are mentioned in the Introduction, there being various ways of making it on the same island. It is important that the fish be fresh, mature, and of varied types.

Time of Consumption ANY TIME OF THE YEAR   Recommended for LUNCH OR DINNER
Recipe for 6 TO 8 PEOPLE   Preparation Time ABOUT 3 HOURS (PREPARING, COOKING AND MAKING THE SAUCE)   Level of Difficulty EASY
Recommended Wine WHITE OF QUALITY, FROM PICO

INGREDIENTS

For the broth:
- 2 kg of various types of fish
- 3 tomatoes
- 4 cloves of garlic
- 1 large onion
- parsley
- home baked bread
- salt, to taste

For the sauce:
- chopped parsley (plenty)
- 3 leeks
- 3 tablespoons of wine vinegar
- 4 tablespoons of good wine, Red or White
- 1 teaspoon of saffron
- water

1 Prepare the fish, cutting it into thick steaks. Clean the tomatoes of the skin and the seeds and cut them into quarters; cut the onion into segments and the leeks into slices.

2 In a wide pan, place enough water to cook the fish and to make the broth; add the onion, leeks, tomatoes and salt (do not add the salt to the fish).

3 Allow to boil until the onion and the tomatoes are cooked. Only then is the fish added, taking care to cook it and not to crumble it into pieces. When it is done, but still firm, add a sprig of parsley, with the heat already off. In the meantime, make the sauce.

4 Parsley sauce for the fish: in a mortar place salt, garlic cloves and chopped parsley. Grind well (crush it).

5 Pour into a bowl into which is added vinegar, wine and water until the quantity is sufficient to marinate the fish, as well as the potatoes that are served with it.

6 Remove the fish onto a serving platter and season with the abovementioned sauce.

7 Cut slices of bread into a bowl and pour the sauce over them, with all the ingredients from the boil (tomato, onion, leeks), but in such a way as not to overly soak them. Decorate with parsley little sprigs.

TIPS AND TRICKS

- The broth is usually drunk from little clay bowls, but in that case, it must be drained. Serve this dish with boiled potatoes and cornbread.

FENNEL SOUP

(TERCEIRA)

The fennel with which this soup is made does not have those great bulbs that are usually found on sale. It is harvested when it has relatively thin branches and very green, fine foliage; the majority of times it grows without being planted or treated, right by the pathways. It has a strong aroma which is appreciated by many.

Time of Consumption NORMALLY IN THE WINTER   *Recommended for* LUNCH OR DINNER
(COULD SERVE AS A MEAL)   *Recipe for* 6 PEOPLE
Preparation Time CBOUT 3 HOURS   *Level of Difficulty* EASY
Recommended Wine REGIONAL RED OF QUALITY

INGREDIENTS
- *1/2 kg of kidney beans*
- *1/2 kg of salted pork meat (for at least 2 days, even at home)*
- *200 g toucinho entremeado, also salted*
- *100 g regional linguiça*
- *1 bunch of fennel, finely cut*
- *2 sweet potatoes*
- *2 normal potatoes, from the land*
- *bolo de panela*

1 Cook the beans, pre-soaked the day before, and reduce to a purée.

2 Bring to the heat and introduce the fennel and the meats. Let it cook.

3 When everything is almost cooked, add the potatoes and the *Bolos de Panela*, which will cook simultaneously. Let the flavour intensify.

4 Serve the soup in a bowl; the meats, the potatoes and the *Bolos de Panela* are served on a separate plate.

TIPS AND TRICKS
- *The Bolos de Panela are not essential. But if you want to make them, here is the recipe: in a bowl place corn flour and let it scald with boiling water seasoned with salt. Do not drench too much. Sprinkle with wheat flour and cover with a plate. When warm, shape with your hands into balls, which are then placed in the pan, to cook.*

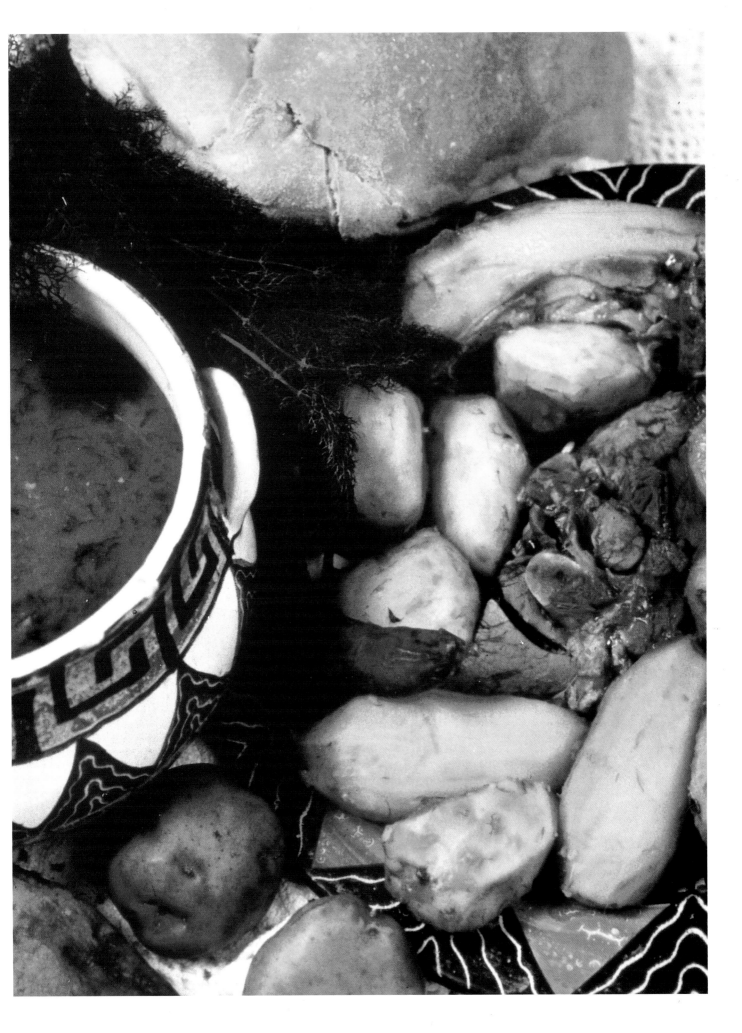

MILK BREAD SOUP

(S. MIGUEL)

On these islands, the bread soups or açordas were often the meal of those who had very little and who were made content with little, saying: "look, I made a little bread soup or açorda". Many times made merely with garlic and, if by chance the chicken had laid some eggs, one would also go into the bread soup or açorda. So were many a meal spent, in this way. Nowadays, this is not so frequent, so that we can now hear: "Goodness, I am yearning for a bread soup or açorda…" Various bread soups or açordas are made: of limpets, of yams, of fish and so on…with whatever the imagination can came up.

Time of Consumption ALL YEAR ROUND　　Recommended for LUNCH OR DINNER
Recipe for 4 PEOPLE　　Preparation Time 1 HOUR　Level of Difficulty EASY
Recommended Wine REGIONAL RED OR WHITE

INGREDIENTS
- 1 medium onion
- 1 litre of milk
- 2 tablespoons of oil
- 1/2 litre of water
- salt, to taste
- white pepper, powdered
- 1 teaspoon saffron
- 2 slices of cornbread
- 2 slices of wheat bread
- 150 g São Jorge cheese
- 4 eggs (optional)

1 Chop the onion and sauté in oil, until transparent.

2 Add the milk and the water, and season with salt, pepper and saffron.

3 Place the bread torn by hand into little pieces and the São Jorge cheese cut into little squares into a bowl. (Another type of cheese may be used, but in the olden days this was the one that was used.)

4 Should eggs be desired, these must be poached on the side.

5 Pour the broth over the bread. Smother with the actual lid of the bowl. Before being served, the eggs will be placed on top of the bread soup or açorda.

TIPS AND TRICKS
- The onion must be finely chopped so as not to be felt when the bread soup or açorda is being enjoyed.

STUFFED SAURELS

Saurel is the name that, in the Azores, is given to the horse-mackerel, which in continental Portugal is only applied to the large saurels. Here, it is known as young or small saurel and well-developed saurel.

Time of Consumption ALL YEAR ROUND   Recommended for LUNCH OR DINNER
Recipe for 4 PEOPLE   Preparation Time 2 HOURS   Level of Difficulty EASY
Recommended Wine WHITE OF QUALITY

INGREDIENTS

- 24 saurels
- 6 bread rolls
- 1 slice of cornbread (optional)
- 2 small onions
- 3 garlic cloves
- 2 tablespoons tomato pulp
- 3 tablespoons vinegar
- 2 tablespoons olive oil
- 1 teaspoon colorau (paprika-like)
- 2 tablespoons of ground pepper paste
- chopped parsley
- 1 egg
- salt, to taste
- pepper, to taste
- corn flour to crumb, as needed
- oil to fry, as needed

1 Open the saurels down the middle (remove the heads, and with a nail, remove the spine), wash and dry them.

2 Season with vinegar, salt, chopped garlic, pepper, ground pepper paste and colorau. Mix them and cover the saurel fillets with this seasoning for more or less 1 hour.

3 In the meantime, prepare the stuffing: soak the bread in lukewarm milk.

4 In a frying pan sauté the onion, the garlic, the ground pepper paste and the tomato pulp. Simmer to let the flavour intensify.

5 Squeeze the bread, adding it to the sautéed mixture, mix and add the egg, the chopped parsley and the salt. Mix it all well and let it simmer to bring out the flavour. Let cool until ready to be worked with again.

6 Drain the already seasoned fillets. On a fillet, with the skin facing down, place a flattened portion of the stuffing, covering this with another fillet, this time with the skin facing up.

7 Thus arranged in layers, pass the fillets through corn flour and fry.

TIPS AND TRICKS

- *The oil should not be too hot to fry properly. It can be served with boiled potatoes and salad. The ground malaguetta (piri-piri) pepper paste is widely used condiment in the Azores, this being obtained from the more or less hot malaguetta (piri-piri), which are crushed and seasoned with salt. In order to preserve well, the resulting paste must be placed into well-closed jar.*

LIMPET SARRABULHO

There are many recipes for limpets: grilled, with sauce, limpets with Afonso sauce, bread with limpet stuffing, limpet rice, etc. There are also those who eat them raw. One could say that there are recipes for all tastes. The one presented here was obtained in São Jorge.

Time of Consumption DURING LIMPET HARVEST TIME   *Recommended for* LUNCH OR DINNER   *Recipe for* 4 PEOPLE   *Preparation Time* 1 HOUR
Level of Difficulty EASY   *Recommended Wine* REGIONAL RED OR WHITE

INGREDIENTS
- 2 kg limpets
- 3 slices of cornbread
- 3 onions
- 4 garlic cloves
- 2 tablespoons of olive oil
- 1 tablespoon malaguetta (piri-piri) paste
- 1 teaspoon crushed pepper
- chopped parsley
- 1 tablespoon lemon juice

1 Scald the limpets with boiling water and cover them so that they emerge from the shells. Drain them and reserve the water.

2 Crush the unshelled limpets and, for each cup of crushed limpets, use 2 of crumbled and crustless cornbread.

3 Sauté the onions and the chopped garlic, in the olive oil, without frying too much.

4 Add the crumbled bread and simmer to let the flavour intensify. If necessary, add a little of the reserved limpet water, sieved though a sieve. Season with the malaguetta (piri-piri) paste and the pepper.

5 Finally add the crushed limpets and plenty of chopped parsley and the lemon juice. Taste and rectify the seasoning.

TIPS AND TRICKS
- When the limpets are added toss the onion, bread and seasonings mixture only once, as the limpets become tough if they are placed too long over the heat.

FISH WITH SAUCE FROM THE VINTAGE (GRACIOSA)

This is an old recipe from Graciosa. It should be mentioned that the fish that was most used in the past was the conger (sea-eel), scaled and salted. At any time of the year this fish was available at home and was used, but its specific season was during the grape-gathering season. Around then, bits of tomato and some bunches of black grape, of great odours, that were squeezed, were combined. It was all boiled and only then was it poured over the fish and the potatoes.

Time of Consumption ANY SEASON   Recommended for LUNCH
Recipe for 4 PEOPLE   Preparation Time 1 HOUR (AFTER FRYING THE FISH)
Level of Difficulty EASY   Recommended Wine WHITE WINE FROM GRACIOSA

INGREDIENTS

- 1,5 kg fish
- 2 garlic heads
- 1 teaspoon saffron
- 1 teaspoon colorau (paprika-like)
- 1/2 coffee spoon of cumin
- 1 swig of vinegar
- oil to fry, as needed
- salt (a little)
- water

1 Sprinkle the fish with salt, as usual.

2 While the fish is being fried, peel and finely chop the garlic, in order to be better crushed in the mortar. Place in a ceramic or heavy glass bowl, adding the saffron, the colorau, and the cumin. Mix well with a wooden spoon.

3 Place the fried fish in the platter where it will be served. At the end, the frying oil is mixed to remove the residues of the fish that was fried, from the bottom of the pan.

4 In the garlic mixture, carefully add the boiling oil (as it tends to rise) and mix well. Next, add the vinegar to taste and a little water, so as to obtain the quantity and consistency required to pour over the fish, and even to serve on the side. There are those who pour this sauce over the boiled potatoes, which are normally served with this dish.

TIPS AND TRICKS

- If you use salted and scaled conger, it should be placed in water without using any salt.

OCTOPUS A LA MODE DE LAGES

(PICO)

Of the many octopus recipes that exist in the archipelago, normally stewed or roasted in the oven, all of them delicious, we chose this one.

Time of Consumption SUMMER AT THE FEASTS IN THE PARISH   Recommended for LUNCH
Recipe for 4 PEOPLE   Preparation Time COOKING OF LONG DURATION
Level of Difficulty EASY   Recommended Wine WHITE OR RED WINE OF QUALITY

INGREDIENTS
- 3 kg octopus
- 3 onions
- 4 garlic cloves
- 2 tablespoons of lard
- 1 bay leaf
- 1 malaguetta (piri-piri)
- 1 litre of wine, red or red
- 2 tablespoons of tomato pulp
- parsley

1 Cut the octopus into little bits and, after being cut, drain it well in order to remove any water it may contain.

2 Cut the onion and the garlic into fine slices.

3 Put the lard in the pan where you will be cooking. Next, place the onion, garlic, bay leaf, and the octopus in layers. In one of the layers place the malaguetta (piri-piri), that was previously seeded. On top, place the tomato pulp and the wine which are to barely cover the octopus. If necessary, an additional amount is added until the octopus is tender. The pot is to be shaken from time to time.

4 When the octopus is almost cooked, a tied sprig of parsley is to be placed on top, which is to be removed before serving.

5 Already on the serving platter, sprinkle with chopped parsley.

TIPS AND TRICKS
- If the octopus is prepared as soon as it comes from the sea, it must be well bashed (beaten), in order to cook better. If frozen octopus is used, it is already much more tender. Normally salt is not used. It may be served with white boiled rice, bolo do Pico or cornbread.

GROUPER in GARLIC AND WINE SAUCE (TERCEIRA)

This recipe was collected from the island of Terceira, and it was impossible to determine if it a traditional recipe only on this island. It is very pleasant and, if well seasoned, it becomes a very tasty dish.

Time of Consumption ALL YEAR ROUND　　Recommended for LUNCH
Recipe for 4 PEOPLE　　Preparation Time 1 AND A HALF HOURS
Level of Difficulty EASY　　Recommended Wine WHITE FROM GRACIOSA

INGREDIENTS
- 1,5 kg medium groupers
- 8 laminated garlic cloves
- 1 tablespoon malaguetta (piri-piri) paste
- 1 teaspoon colorau (paprika-like)
- salt, to taste
- 1 bay leaf
- 1/2 litre white wine
- 2 boiled eggs
- oil, as needed
- chopped parsley

1　After being cleaned, the fish is cut into not very thin steaks and is seasoned with salt, garlic, bay leaf, malaguetta (piri-piri) paste, *colorau* and wine. It is to be placed for one or two days in the fridge, stirring a couple of times.

2　On the day of preparation, drain and reserve the marinade liquid.

3　Fry the fish in hot oil which is then placed on the serving platter.

4　Pour the garlic wine marinade (*vinha d'alhos*) liquid, thinly, into the oil where it was fried and allow to reduce a little.

5　Strain and pour over the fried fish. Sprinkle with chopped boiled egg and parsley.

TIPS AND TRICKS
- *Before pouring the garlic wine marinade (vinha d'alhos) liquid in the oil, scrape well in order to release any fish residues.*

DRIED MACKEREL WITH RAW SAUCE

This recipe is served as an 'appetiser', as the seasoning is tasty. Dried scaled mackerel is greatly appreciated. Those who go to sea, prepare it for their own consumption or for resale. Of course, this is not the only recipe of dried mackerel that is known.

Time of Consumption ALL YEAR ROUND   Recommended for APPETISER
Recipe for VARIOUS PLEOPLE   Preparation Time 1 AND A HALF HOURS
Level of Difficulty EASY   Recommended Wine REGIONAL RED OR WHITE

INGREDIENTS
- 2 dried mackerels
- oil, as needed
- 10 garlic cloves
- 1 large onion
- 1 tablespoon malaguetta (piri-piri) paste
- chopped parsley
- 2 dl olive oil
- 1/2 dl vinegar
- salt, to taste

1 Cut the mackerel into bits and place it, in water, for 24 hours.

2 Scald it with boiling water, drain it, dry it and fry it in oil. Place it on the serving platter.

3 Finely chop the garlic and onion, add the olive oil and vinegar, malagueta (piri-piri) paste and chopped parsley.

4 Taste. Rectify the seasoning, taking into account the salt of the mackerel.

5 Pour this over the mackerel, which is normally served cold.

TIPS AND TRICKS
- *I you wish to prepare the mackerel at home, open the fish down the middle and place layers of salt and of the open mackerel, in a bowl or box of plastic. Leave like this for 2 days and after this period, take it out, shake off the loose salt, and place them in the sun, to dry. This appetiser may be made the whole year, as the mackerels, after being dried, can be frozen.*

SAURELS WITH GREEN SAUCE

(S. MIGUEL)

This is yet another saurel recipe and is also from São Miguel. It is very tasty and easy, besides being practical, as it can be eaten both hot and cold, and even from one day to the next.

Time of Consumption ANY TIME OF THE YEAR   *Recommended for* LUNCH
Recipe for 4 PEOPLE   *Preparation Time* 1 HOUR PLUS THE TIME FOR THE GARLIC WINE
MARINADE   *Level of Difficulty* EASY   *Recommended Wine* WHITE FROM THE REGION

INGREDIENTS
- 1/2 kg saurels
- 4 garlic cloves
- salt, to taste
- 1 tablespoon ground pepper paste
- 3 Galego lemons (or limes or sour oranges)
- corn flour, as needed
- oil for frying, as needed

For the sauce:
- 2 Cortume onions (in vinegar and spices)
- chopped parsley, plenty
- 1 chopped garlic clove
- 1 glass of olive oil
- 1 tablespoon vinegar (from the onions)
- 1 small malaguetta (piri-piri)
- 1 coffee spoon saffron

1 After having cleaned the saurels, make a garlic wine marinade (vinha d'alhos) with the chopped garlic, salt, pepper paste, which were crushed in a mortar and to which, after well crushed and mixed, the lemon juice is added. Rub the saurels in this. Leave to marinade for 2 hours.

2 After this period of time, shake the fish off and fry the saurels in oil, covered in corn flour (in the olden days lard was used to fry).

3 While the fish is frying, make the green sauce with the finely chopped onions (without making it pasty), parsley, finely chopped garlic clove, olive oil, vinegar, chopped malaguetta (piri-piri) and saffron.

4 As the saurels are fried, so they are covered by the sauce and placed on the serving platter. Pour the remaining sauce over all the saurels.

5 Cover up if they are to be eaten at the next meal.

TIPS AND TRICKS
- When using the pepper paste, one must be careful with the salt used as, as was previously mentioned in another recipe, this paste is preserved with salt. It may be served with potatoes boiled in their skins or with yams.

OVEN-BAKED ALBACORE

(LAGES, FLORES)

In France, the albacore is one of 5 species of tuna. In the USA, albacore is the name given to fresh white tuna, while our albacore is known as yellowskin. It is fished practically throughout the whole year in tropical and equatorial waters. In the Azores, one finds fresh albacore more easily and at certain times of the year on the islands of Faial and Flores. It should be prepared with the same care with which fresh tuna is prepared.

Time of Consumption FROM SPRING (FRESH ALBACORE SEASON) *Recommended for* LUNCH OR DINNER *Recipe for* 4 PEOPLE *Preparation Time* 3 HOURS *Level of Difficulty* EASY *Recommended Wine* WHITE FROM PICO

INGREDIENTS
- *1,5 k albacore*
- *3 tablespoons oil*
- *2 onions*
- *3 garlic cloves*
- *2 tomatoes*
- *1 tablespoon capsicum paste*
- *1 tablespoon malaguetta (piri-piri) paste*
- *1/2 coffee spoon of cumin*
- *1 tablespoon tomato pulp*
- *chopped parsley*
- *1/2 litre white wine*
- *salt, to taste*

1 When purchasing a whole albacore, cut the head and remove the side bones. skinning is much easier this way. Remove the middle bone as well and cut into bits as if for *torresmos*.

2 Without any seasoning, colour in oil and place on a tray.

3 In the same oil where the fish was coloured, sauté the onion and chopped garlic till golden; afterwards, add the tomato in bits, the capsicum and malaguetta (piri-piri) pastes, the cumin and the parsley. A very thick mixture will be the result.

4 Pour the wine and only then, season with salt.

5 Place potatoes, cut into small cubes, around the albacore in the tray. Taste to check the seasoning. If necessary, add a little more wine or water, according to the taste it already has.

6 Place in the oven. From time to time, place a couple of spoonfuls of the gravy over the fish and over the potatoes.

TIPS AND TRICKS
- It may also be served with sweet potatoes cooked separately.

CLAMS

(S. JORGE)

These clams, as may be attested by the photograph, are of an extraordinary size; and the same might be said for their taste. They are cultivated in the Caldeira de Santo Cristo, in São Jorge, the only place in the archipelago where such molluscs are cultivated. They experience closed seasons but, if during authorised seasons they are gathered and frozen, they are also kept alive and ready for cooking when placed in slated water, or better still, in sea water.

Time of Consumption FROZEN, ANY TIME OF THE YEAR
Recommended for STARTERS   Recipe for 4 PEOPLE   Preparation Time DELAYED
BY THE WAITING PERIOD TO REMOVE THE SAND   Level of Difficulty EASY
Recommended Wine WHITE WINE FROM BISCOITOS

INGREDIENTS
- 2 kg clams
- 2 onions
- 4 garlic cloves
- 2 ripe tomatoes
- 1 tablespoon malaguetta (piri-piri) paste
- chopped parsley

1 Make an onion and tomato mixture. Sauté the chopped garlic and onion, to which, once ready, are added the tomatoes in little pieces and chopped parsley.

2 Add the clams and the malaguetta (piri-piri) paste next. Shake the pan until all the clams are open.

3 Taste the sauce and check the seasonings. Normally, there is no need to add salt.

4 Place on a tray just before serving.

TIPS AND TRICKS
- *The clams must be placed in salted water to release the sand. This water must be changed at least 3 times. It is said that for the São Jorge clams to be tastier that a cloth should be passed over them, one by one, to remove the taste of the mud they might still have. Handicrafts, like painting and even figurines, are made with the bigger shells.*

GROUPER PIES

(TERCEIRA)

These pies of exquisite taste are loaded with tradition and are greatly appreciated. These were resorted to during Lent, due to the prohibition of meat consumption. There were even experts in their preparation, as we have to admit that they laborious and require patience and know-how.

Time of Consumption ANY TIME OF THE YEAR   Recommended for MEALS
Recipe for 5 PEOPLE   Preparation Time LENGTHY   Level of Difficulty LABORIOUS RECIPE
Recommended Wine WHITE WINE FROM BISCOITOS

INGREDIENTS

For the dough:
- 500 g flour
- 100 g sugar
- 175 g butter (melted)
- 100 g lard (melted)
- 2 eggs
- 1 coffee spoon cinnamon
- salt, to taste

For the filling:
- 1,5 kg grouper
- 1/2 litre white wine, good
- water and salt, as needed
- 1 swig of vinegar
- 8 chopped garlic cloves
- 1 onion
- 1 teaspoon pepper corns
- parsley
- 1 tablespoon lard
- 1 tablespoon olive oil
- 1 teaspoon malaguetta (piri-piri) paste
- 8 pitted olives
- 125 g nut kernel
- boiling water
- 1 egg yellow
- stuffed olives

DOUGH:

1 Mix all the ingredients, kneading and working the dough well. Generally this work is done the day before, leaving the dough in a bowl covered with a cloth.

FILLING:

1 Also on the day before, cut the fish and place it into a garlic wine marinade made with the wine, water, salt, vinegar, garlic, onion in small bits, peppercorns and a tied-up sprig of parsley.

2 On the following day, remove the fish, strain the sauce to which the lard, olive oil, malaguetta (piri-piri) paste and salt are added.

3 In this sauce cook the fish, slowly.

4 Once cooked, remove the fish and cut it into pieces that will fit into the pie moulds.

5 Add the chopped olives and the cut fish into the water from the boiling.

6 Separately, crush the nuts in a mortar, crushing them until they turn into oil. Pour a little boiling water into this dough, which is then strained and added to the previous sauce.

7 Line the pie moulds with the dough, fill with the fish, a spoonful of the sauce and one stuffed olive. Cover with dough, closing the edges firmly, and brushing over with egg yellow.

8 Place in the oven on a baking tray.

9 With the rest of the dough, make snail-shaped rolls that are also brushed over with egg and are also placed in the oven.

10 When the pies begin to turn golden, remove them, make a small perforation in the centre of each one and, with a thin funnel, pour more sauce in, covering these with the 'snails' of dough. Place them again in the oven to finish baking.

TORRESMOS IN A GARLIC AND WINE SAUCE (S. MIGUEL)

This recipe is made with pork meat, from the sparerib, thus also being known as torresmos de "cabinho". It is one of those recipes that, with slight differences, are done on all the islands. In the olden days it was only done during the period when the pig was killed. It is also done now at the feasts in the parishes that take place throughout the year.

Time of Consumption ALL YEAR ROUND **Recommended for** MAIN DISH
Recipe for 8 PEOPLE **Preparation Time** LENGTHY PREPARATION
Level of Difficulty EASY PREPARATION **Recommended Wine** RED WINE FROM PICO

INGREDIENTS
- 4 kg pork sparerib
- 750 g liver
- 8 tablespoons malaguetta (piri-piri) paste
- 1/2 litre red wine
- 1 coffee spoon white pepper and the same of black pepper
- 10 chopped or crushed garlic cloves
- 500 g lard
- 3 tablespoons colorau (paprika-like)
- salt, to taste

1 Clean the meat of excessive skin and fat and cut it, leaving 2 chops (or ribs) for each *torresmo*.

2 Clean and cut the liver into little bits.

3 Make a garlic wine marinade (*vinha d'alhos*) with the malaguetta (piri-piri) paste (careful with the salt), garlic, peppers, wine and salt (if needed), and place the meat and the liver in it.

4 Bring the meat to the boil with the garlic wine marinade (*vinha d'alhos*) in a heavy-based pan, to avoid sticking. Add the lard and allow to boil over strong heat at the beginning, reducing it later. Mix once in a while.

5 When beginning to dry out, and the meat is becoming tender, add the liver, always at a more reduced heat, and allow to finish cooking. Avoid letting the liver overcook, as it will become tough. Allow the flavours to intensify.

6 Taste, and rectify the seasonings to taste and, when practically ready, add the *colorau*, mixing well and leaving it a further 5 minutes on the heat.

7 Leave the covered *torresmos* to rest 10 to 15 minutes and serve.

TIPS AND TRICKS
- *With the remnants at the bottom of the pan, called pé de torresmo, make some "dry oven cakes" (bolos secos de forno), by throwing boiling water into the torresmo remnants and adding corn flour. Taste and mould, by hand, into flat cakes, that are baked in the oven.*

DESCAÍDA

Collected at the Fazenda do Nordeste, in São Miguel, this is one of those recipes that may be made with whatever one has in the house, especially in rural parishes. It may seem a little simple, but it is quite a tasty recipe.

Time of Consumption ALL YEAR ROUND   Recommended for LUNCH OR DINNER
Recipe for 4 PEOPLE   Preparation Time HOUR AND A HALF   Level of Difficulty EASY
Recommended Wine REGIONAL RED

INGREDIENTS
- 1/2 chicken
- 1/2 kg chicken giblets
- 1 onion
- 3 garlic cloves
- 1 parsley sprig
- 1 tablespoon pepper broth
- 1 tablespoon lard
- 1 coffee spoon cinnamon
- half of a home made-type bread, chopped
- salt, to taste

1 Boil the giblets and the chicken in water seasoned with salt, in combination with the chopped onion and garlic, pepper broth, cinnamon and lard.

2 When everything is cooked, cut the giblets into little pieces and shred the chicken.

3 "Nibble at" the bread, including the crust, and pour into the broth with the chicken and the chopped giblets. Mix well in order to combine it all together.

4 Taste, to rectify the seasoning.

TIPS AND TRICKS
· One may, according to each one's own preference, leave more or less liquid.

MOLHA À LA MODE DE PICO

While this recipe was collected in Faial, it was nonetheless referred to me that it was according to the tradition in Pico. However, I have already also enjoyed it in Faial as being typical of the latter.

Time of Consumption ANY TIME OF THE YEAR   Recommended for LUNCH OR DINNER   Recipe for 6 PEOPLE   Preparation Time 4 HOURS Level of Difficulty EASY   Recommended Wine RED FROM PICO

INGREDIENTS
- 4 kg beef with bone
- 1/2 litre white wine
- 2 tablespoons lard
- 3 large onions
- 8 garlic cloves
- 2 chopped malaguetta (piri-piri)
- 2 tablespoons tomato pulp
- 1 tablespoon Jamaican peppercorns
- 1 bay leaf
- 1/2 coffee spoon powdered cumin
- 1 cinnamon stick

1 Cut the meat into medium portions, mix with salt, some crushed garlic cloves and malaguetta (piri-piri), even rubbing it all in with your hands. Let it rest thus for a couple of hours.

2 Make an onion and tomato mixture. Sauté the onion, garlic and lard. When golden, add the tomato pulp, cumin, Jamaican pepper, mixing all the time; add the wine and the cinnamon stick. Boil a little.

3 Add the meat and let it simmer gently for more or less 2 hours or until it is cooked. If it begins to dry, add a little bit of water, thus also making some gravy. Place a sprig of parsley.

4 Taste to rectify the seasoning and allow the flavours to intensify.

TIPS AND TRICKS
- As is generally known, one should always let any cooked dish rest, covered, after its preparation is done, to let the flavours finish intensifying. This molha is presented on a large plate, with boiled potatoes all around.

SOAKED LIVER

(CORVO)

Up until some years ago, the strong dishes of this island were made from pork meat. Nowadays other meats are already used.

Time of Consumption CURRENTLY ALL YEAR ROUND   *Recommended for* SIDE DISHES OR APPETISERS, ACCORDING TO THE OCCASION   *Recipe for 4* PLEOPLE (IF AS A MAIN DISH)
Preparation Time LENGTHY   *Level of Difficulty* EASY
Recommended Wine REGIONAL RED

INGREDIENTS
- 250 g boneless pork meat
- 2 pork tongues
- 2 pork hearts
- 250 g pork liver
- 6 garlic cloves
- 2 tablespoons capsicum paste
- 1 tablespoon Jamaican peppercorns
- 1 coffee spoon cumin
- 1 coffee spoon crushed pepper
- 1,1/2 dl vinegar
- 1/2 dl white wine
- 500 g lard

1 Cut the meat, the heart and the tongues into not very little portions.

2 Place them in a garlic wine marinade (*vinha d'alhos*) with garlic, salt, capsicum paste, Jamaican peppercorns, cumin, pepper, vinegar and wine.

3 Cut the liver into smaller portions and season separately, like the meats, but without the wine and the vinegar. Leave to marinate for 2 days.

4 After this period, the meats are drained and are fried in lard, in a heavy-based pan.

5 When the meats are fried, add the liver, which will fry for only a short while so that it does not become tough. The liquid of the garlic wine marinade (*vinha d'alhos*) is not used.

6 This may be eaten at the next meal or it may be kept in casks, covering it all up properly with the lard in which it was all fried. Afterwards, as often as one wants, the desired quantity may be taken out into a frying pan, warmed up and served.

TIPS AND TRICKS
- *The meat chosen for this dish was that of pork fillets. It may be served with boiled sweet potato, corn bread and even fried eggs.*

COZINHADA of PORK

This recipe, with a few alterations, appears in more than one island, having always as its base the pork meat, the firm green cabbage and potatoes. The pork cozinhada is usually made on Thursdays and on Sundays.

Time of Consumption ALL YEAR ROUND   Recommended for MAIN DISH
Recipe for 4 PEOPLE   Preparation Time 3 WEEKS FOR THE SALT CURING AND 2 HOURS FOR THE PREPARATION *Level of Difficulty* EASY *Recommended Wine* REGIONAL RED OF QUALITY

INGREDIENTS
- *2 kg pork meats (ribs, vertebras and* toucinho entremeado)
- *1 bunch of cabbage*
- *2 new potatoes*
- *2 sweet potatoes*
- *salt, plenty*

1 Three weeks in advance, the salt curing is done (layer of salt, layer of meats; layer of salt, layer of meats).

2 The day before the preparation of the dish, place it all in water, changing it ABOUT 3 times.

3 On the day, scald the meats with boiling water which is then discarded.

4 In a different water, place the meats together with the cabbage, cut into thick strips, and leave to boil until tender.

5 When it is all cooked, remove enough broth to cook the potatoes.

6 Serve on a large plate, with the cabbage in the middle and, all around, the sliced meats and the potatoes.

TIPS AND TRICKS
- *Firm, well-developed cabbage should be used so that, as it cooks, it does not come undone. This recipe was also known by the name "Pork with cabbage" or "Pork cozido".*

RUMP

(TERCEIRA)

The "alcatra" or rump is a very typical dish from island of Terceira, cooked in an unglazed clay bowl, this being the last dish to be served in the "Service" or "Funções". It is made with beef, not very tender and with bone, so that as it takes longer to cook, its flavour is intensified and the sauce thickened. Preferably made in a firewood oven, it is already made in a gas oven, letting it cook and its flavour intensify for longer than a day.

Time of Consumption ANY TIME OF THE YEAR   Recommended for MAIN DISH
Recipe for 6 PEOPLE   Preparation Time ABOUT 4 HOURS   Level of Difficulty
EASY   Recommended Wine REGIONAL WINE OF BISCOITOS

INGREDIENTS
- 2 kg rump, with bone
- 150 g smoked toucinho
- 1 portion of leg of beef, of inferior quality
- 4 tablespoons lard
- 4 large onions
- 4 garlic cloves
- 1 bay leaf
- salt, to taste
- 1 dessert spoon of black peppercorns
- 1 dessert spoon of Jamaican peppercorns
- red wine, to taste

1 Cut the meat into not so small pieces, cut the onions into slices as well as the garlic and slice the *toucinho* into small strips. Place a spoon of lard and a handful of onion into an unglazed clay bowl.

2 On a separate container, combine the meats, *toucinho*, remaining onion, garlic, peppers, salt, bay leaf and 1 glass of wine. Mix all the ingredients and place them into the clay bowl with the lard and the onion.

3 Add the remaining lard and add more wine.

4 In the olden days, as one placed the rump or *alcatra* in the firewood oven it was covered with a tin or aluminium lid. Nowadays, aluminium foil paper is used..

5 Allow to boil some 2 hours, covered. On the next day, return to the oven, uncovered, check for salt and add more wine if necessary. As it cooks. it will become golden.

TIPS AND TRICKS
- It is not convenient to cover completely with the wine, as, with the melting of the lard and of the toucinho, the resulting sauce may spill out. It should be served in the clay bowl and still boiling. The proper accompaniment is massa sovada.

ROASTED MEAT
OF THE MANADAS (S. JORGE)

This recipe of roasted meat, served with massa sovada, *was taken to the Empires and distributed among the people that passed through. The use of tender meat is not recommended for this recipe.*

Time of Consumption SERVED AT THE TIME OF THE FESTIVITIES OF THE HOLY GHOST
Recommended for MEAL   *Recipe for* 6 PESSOAS   *Preparation Time* 3 HOURS
Level of Difficulty EASY   *Recommended Wine* REGIONAL WINE OF BISCOITOS

INGREDIENTS
- 1,5 kg leg meat with bone
- 6 garlic cloves
- salt, to taste
- 2 tablespoons malaguetta (piri-piri) paste
- 1 teaspoon colorau (paprika-like)
- 2 large onions
- 150 g regional linguiça
- 100 g smoked toucinho
- 1 teaspoon Jamaican peppercorns
- 1 litre white wine
- 1 beer
- butter

1 Clean the meat of skins and fats.

2 Crush and mix the garlic, *colorau*, malaguetta (piri-piri) paste, salt (carefully) in a mortar, all well-crushed.

3 Rub the meat very well with this paste and allow to rest some 3 hours.

4 In a clay or enamel baking tray, place a layer of sliced onions and garlic, the *linguiça*, the *toucinho* cut into bits and the Jamaican pepper.

5 Place the meat over that and pour wine. Place in the oven, which in the olden days, used to always be made of firewood, taking more or less 3 hours to roast.

6 As it begins to dry out, continue adding more wine.

7 From time to time, turn the meat, spreading it with the butter on each of its sides.

8 When half-cooked, add the entire beer. Taste, and if need be, rectify the seasoning. Allow the flavours to intensify and the sauce to thicken.

TIPS AND TRICKS
- When it has to be done in a gas oven, it takes some time to cook. It should be covered with aluminium foil paper, when it begins to become too golden.

RICE RISSOLES

(GRACIOSA)

These rissoles, already currently being marketed in proper packaging, are, together with the queijadas from Graciosa, the visiting card of that island.

Time of Consumption AT ANY TIME OF THE YEAR   Recommended for DESSERT
Recipe for 12 PEOPLE   Preparation Time ONE HOUR AND A HALF
Level of Difficulty AVERAGE   Recommended Wine APERITIF FROM THE WINE CELLAR
CO-OPERATIVE SOCIETY OF GRACIOSA

INGREDIENTS

For the dough:
- 500 g flour
- 3 tablespoons sugar
- 1 tablespoon butter
- 2 egg yolks
- water and salt, as needed

For the filling:
- 16 egg yolks
- 500 g sugar
- 125 g almond kernel, peeled and crushed
- 125 g dough of boiled rice
- lemon rind

1 Make the dough by mixing all the ingredients together. Allow to rest for 15 minutes.

2 Boil the rice in a little water and pass through a fine sieve and only then, weigh the required dough quantity.

3 In the meantime, put the sugar to boil on the heat with a little water until it reaches the point of a paste.

4 Add the almond and the rice dough next.

5 Over low heat, bring to the boil, always stirring. Remove from the heat and allow to cool about 10 minutes.

6 Add the already mixed yolks and lemon rind to the previous mixture. Return to the heat, mixing until it thickens and until the bottom of the pan is visible. Cool.

7 Roll out the dough with the rolling pin, as if for *rissoles*, make a wide band, into which little portions of the filling are placed. Fold the dough and, with your fingers, pressing down, make the shape out for the *pastéis* (a little smaller than *rissoles*), which are cut out with a pastry-cutter.

8 Melt a little butter, which is put with a brush or even a finger over the pastéis (not much) and place in the oven.

9 Remove when done (more or less 15 minutes) and sprinkle with powdered sugar.

TIPS AND TRICKS

The oven should be mild. The tray where they are placed is not to be greased. In order to preserve well, a sheet of baking paper could be placed, if needed, between each layer of the pastéis in well-shut boxes.

BRAN PUDDING

(TERCEIRA)

The bran or rolão is what is obtained after the flour is sifted for the second time. It is a fine product, but not as much as the flour. It is known as fine bran bread flour or sêmea.

Time of Consumption AT ANY TIME OF THE YEAR   Recommended for DESSERT
Recipe for 8 PEOPLE   Preparation Time 2 HOURS   Level of Difficulty AVERAGE
Recommended Wine APERITIF FROM BISCOITOS

INGREDIENTS

- 750 g sugar
- 7,5 dl water
- 100 g bran or rolão
- 12 egg yolks
- 3 egg whites
- 1 tablespoon butter
- 125 g almond kernel, peeled, roasted and crushed
- powdered sugar, as needed

1 Dissolve the sugar in the water; bring to the boil to a light point.

2 Allow to cool, adding the almond, butter, the bran or *rolão*, and the lightly beaten egg yolks.

3 Return to the heat just to boiling point.

4 Remove from the heat and, when lukewarm, add the stiffly beaten egg whites.

5 Place in the oven at 180° in a well-greased solid cake mould, for approximately 1 hour and a half. The baking time, however, should be controlled after one hour.

6 Take out of the mould and sprinkle with powdered sugar.

TIPS AND TRICKS

- Try the sugar point, by wetting your fingers in the syrup and by feeling them sticky. For better results, grease the cake mould well, line with baking paper and grease well once again.

GREEN TEA PUDDING
(S. MIGUEL)

This recipe was given to me by the proprietor of the Gorreana cultivations, Mrs Margarida Meireles Gago da Câmara Hintze Mota. It is a very pleasant and easy recipe.

Time of Consumption AT ANY TIME OF THE YEAR   Recommended for DESSERT
Recipe for 8 PEOPLE   Preparation Time 2 HOURS   Level of Difficulty EASY
Recommended Wine WINE LIQUEUR OR HOUSE WINE

INGREDIENTS
- 1/2 litre milk
- 2 tablespoons green tea
- 460 g sugar
- 12 egg yolks
- 2 egg whites

1 Open the tea leaves in the milk, as if it were water.

2 Take a little sugar from the indicated weight required of sugar to melt and brown it and then to caramelize the pudding mould.

3 Beat the egg yolks and the egg whites with the remaining sugar, adding the sieved milk. Mix well.

4 Place in the oven to bake in *bain marie*.

TIPS AND TRICKS
· You could grease the mould with butter, before covering it with the burnt sugar.

ESPÉCIES

This recipe is one (of five or six) of those recipes that have passed through my hands about which whoever gave it to me declared that it is the most authentic or the oldest. They vary mainly in terms of spices, as the way of making them is identical. It is one of the great specialities of the island of São Jorge.

Time of Consumption AT ANY TIME OF THE YEAR   Recommended for TEATIME OR DESSERT
Recipe for 12 PEOPLE   Preparation Time QUITE LENGTHY
Level of Difficulty HARD   Recommended Wine APERITIF FROM BISCOITOS

INGREDIENTS

For the dough:
- 1 kg flour
- 125 g butter
- 2 eggs
- 1 pinch of salt
- 1 tablespoon of lard

For the filling:
- 1 kg sugar
- 1 egg
- 500 g fine breadcrumb flour
- thin skins of 2 lemons, boiled and grated
- 70 g crushed sweet herbs
- 125 g butter
- 40 g cinnamon
- 1 coffee spoon of crushed white pepper

1 Let us start with the filling: beat the sugar with the egg.

2 In a non-stick pan, place 1/4 litre of water, the lemon skins, cinnamon, pepper, butter, sweet herbs and the sugar with the egg.

3 Bring to the heat, mixing until it thickens a little..

4 Pass through a sieve, and when lukewarm, mix in the flour (at times, not all of it is put in).

5 Return to the heat to cook and to thicken in order to shape. Keep from one day to the next.

6 The dough is made by mixing and kneading well all the ingredients.

7 Shape the filling into a few little rolls, which are then cut to the size of the *Espécies*.

8 With a rolling pin, roll out the dough and cut into thin strips of about 6cm wide, making some cuts with the pastry-cutter; in the middle, place the little filling rolls in the centre, fold over that, press down and cut with the pastry-cutter. Give it the shape of a horse-shoe, applying gentle pressure between the cuts, so that they open while they bake.

9 Place in the oven to bake, on a greased tray.

TIPS AND TRICKS

- *To shape the little rolls of filling, which were called "bichos" in the olden days, you can grease your hands with butter.*

DONA AMÉLIA CAKES
(TERCEIRA)

It is said that when Queen Amélia visited the island of Terceira that some cakes were made that Her Majesty enjoyed so much that they were named after her. There are also variations of this recipe. Which would be the authentic one?

Time of Consumption AT ANY TIME OF THE YEAR   Recommended for TEATIME OR DESSERT
Recipe for 8 PEOPLE   Preparation Time HOUR AND A HALF   Level of Difficulty EASY
Recommended Beverage WINE APERITIF, LIQUEUR, TEA OR COFFEE

INGREDIENTS
- 250 g maize flour
- 5 whole eggs
- 4 egg yolks
- 1/2 kg sugar
- 1 dessert spoon cinnamon
- 2 tablespoons cane honey
- 225 g melted butter
- 50 g currants
- 80 g crystallized candied citron-peel, chopped

1 Beat the whole eggs with the sugar.

2 Add the egg yolks, continuing to beat.

3 Add the butter in the same way.

4 Mix the flour, cinnamon and the honey next, always mixing.

Finally, add the currants and the citron-peel into the mixture.

5 Pour the mixture into well-greased cup cake moulds, and the cakes are baked in a medium hot oven, under constant control.

TIPS AND TRICKS
· If unable to get cane honey, you may use pure honey. The citron-peel is optional.

MILK LIQUEUR

Around Christmas, it was traditional to make, quite in advance, various homemade liqueurs, destined for the friends who were to come round. These liqueurs, characteristic of the Christmassy period, were tenderly named the "wee of little Jesus" or "o xixi do Menino Jesus". This tradition, with the passing of time and the running around for time, is now starting to disappear, although, it is continued by inviting friends over for the so-called "xixi" that now, at the best of times, is no more than a gin, a whisky or any another purchased drink.

Time of Consumption AROUND CHRISTMAS **Recommended for** AS AN ACCOMPANIMENT TO A SWEET OR DESSERT **Preparation Time** 3 TO 4 WEEKS **Level of Difficulty** EASY

INGREDIENTS
- 1 litre of milk
- 1 litre of alcohol
- 1 lemon in slices
- 1 vanilla pod
- 125 g chocolate, in a bar, broken into pieces
- 1 kg sugar

1 Infuse all the ingredients together, for at least 15 days (but the more days the better), shaking on a daily basis.

2 Prepare a beautiful flask or bottle and with a funnel and filter paper, pour slowly, letting it filter through, which may take a few days.

TIPS AND TRICKS
- CWith the residues that remain in the filter, one can make a delicious pudding, by adding them to syrup made with 500 g sugar (boiled to the point of a paste) and which one allows to boil for a little while. When lukewarm, 8 egg yolks and 4 stiffly beaten egg whites are added, placing it into the oven in a well-greased mould.

CLOUDED EGGS

This pan dessert acts as an after dinner sweet, being served with tea, since the latter was more often served than coffee.

Time of Consumption AT ANY TIME OF THE YEAR   Recommended for DESSERT   Recipe for 8 PEOPLE   Preparation Time MORE OR LESS 1 HOUR AND A HALF   Level of Difficulty EASY
Recommended Beverage TEA

INGREDIENTS
- 500 g sugar
- 7 egg yolks
- 2 eggs
- 1/2 coffee spoon of fine salt
- cinnamon, to taste

1 Make a strong, quite golden, caramel with the sugar.

2 Carefully add the necessary water to make the caramel liquid, and only then, add the eggs and the egg yolks, beaten with the salt.

3 Mix with a wooden spoon, over the heat, in a seesaw motion, making slabs.

4 Let it cook rapidly and pour into a glass bowl, preferably low, sprinkling them with cinnamon.

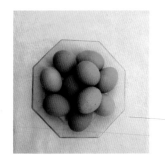

TIPS AND TRICKS
- While mixing with the wooden spoon to make the slabs, you may, according to taste, leave them more or less broken.

CORNUCOPIAS

(TERCEIRA)

This is a sweet that, besides making a beautiful presentation, delights those with a very sweet tooth for, as we shall see, it is a very sweet....sweet.

Time of Consumption AT ANY TIME OF THE YEAR   Recommended for TEATIME OR DESSERT
Recipe for 12 PEOPLE   Preparation Time 2 TO 2 HOURS AND A HALF
Level of Difficulty AVERAGE   Recommended Beverage WINE APERITIF, LIQUEUR, TEA OR COFFEE

INGREDIENTS

- 500 g flour
- 2 dessert spoons butter
- 2 tablespoons lard
- 4 tablespoons sugar
- 2 tablespoons breadcrumbs
- 4 tablespoons almonds, with skins, lightly roasted and crushed

Filling:

ovos moles

1 Mix the flour with the lard, butter, and sugar, moistening with very hot water, sufficient to knead and make mouldable. Leave to rest some 15 minutes.

2 Grease the proper moulds (conical) with butter.

3 Roll out the dough, thinly, cutting triangles that are rolled into the moulds, lightly brushing over them with a lightly beaten egg white, and then rolling them over the breadcrumbs mixed with the almonds.

4 Place in a very hot oven, controlling the baking process.

5 Take out of the moulds and serve filled with ovos moles, which are made with a syrup of 500g sugar and 12 egg yolks.

TIPS AND TRICKS

- The cornucopias must only be filled as close to serving time as possible.

WINES OF THE AZORES

The wines of the Azores are heirs to an ancient vine-growing tradition that dates back to the period of the first colonisers (15th century).

The chronicles mention the presence of wine of the Azores on the vessels that stocked up at Porto das Pipas (Island of Terceira) and which made for the ports in the Indies and overseas.

The Azorean wine sold well, in the 18th century, in America, in the Antilles, in Hamburg and in St Petersburg, even being appreciated by the actual Czars of Russia.

In the 19th century the Azorean wine is exported to Brazil, where it was suggested by doctors as a medicinal product.

The Verdelho strain, which is thought to be from the Mediterranean and which will have been introduced in the 15th century, is one of the best adapted to the Azorean climate and fields, holding out till now.

In the second half of the 19th century, the vines of the Azores were decimated by plagues (*oidium tukeri*, *mildium* and phylloxera), so that the productions fell catastrophically. Hundreds of families were left in total misery, and were forced to take up activities like whale hunting or to emigrate to the USA.

The tradition of quality wines of the Azores is only resumed in the 80's in the last century, with the regrowth of the Verdelho strain and the experimentation of other strains in testing fields set up by official services.

Already in the 90's the Vine-Growing Areas of Biscoitos (island of Terceira), Graciosa and Pico were created.

The wines certified by the CVR-Açores are. Lagido (VLQPRD), of Pico; Brum (VLQPRD), of Biscoitos and Pedras Brancas (VQPRD), of Graciosa.

"Combining a tradition that dates back to the 15th century to knowledge and up-to-date technology, the wines of Azores, reacquire, thus, their place in the wine-cellars of quality". (*Vinhos dos Açores* by Armando Mendes a DRDA edition). Some of the wines of Azores are listed next:

"Pedras Brancas (VQPRD) – Type White – Year 1997 – Region Graciosa – Colour Gold with a bright green shade – Aroma Intense and fruity, with a light smoked hint of flowers and wild bushes - Alcohol 11,6% - Consumption Temperature between 8 and 10°C – Producer/Bottler Adega Cooperativa da Graciosa.

BRUM VQPRD – Type Liqueur-like – Year 1994 – Region Biscoitos – Colour Old gold, with green shades – Aroma Elegant, of dried fruits with a touch of spices and tobacco - Alcohol 17% - Consumption Temperature around 8°C – Producer/Bottler Casa Agrícola Brum Lda.

LAGIDO VQPRD – Type Liqueur-like – Year 1994 – Region Pico – Colour Definitive gold – Aroma Very fine, of cigars, smell of the sea, dried fruits and spices - Alcohol 16,5% - Consumption Temperature around 8°C – Producer/Bottler Cooperativa Vitivinícula da Ilha do Pico

VINHO DA PEDRA – Type White – Year 1999 – Region Biscoitos – Colour Definitive citrine – Aroma Reasonably fruity of *copota* and bergamot- Alcohol 11,5% - Consumption Temperature between 8 and 10°C – Producer/Bottler Adega Coop. dos Biscoitos.

TERRAS DE LAVA – Type White – Year 1998 – Region Pico – Colour Brilliant golden straw – Aroma Intense of wild fruits and honey- Alcohol 11,5% - Consumption Temperature between 8 and 10°C – Producer/Bottler Coop. Vitiv. Da Ilha do Pico.

CURRAL ATLANTIS – Type White – Year 1998 – Region Pico – Colour Pale straw with green tonalities – Aroma Lightly fruity and evanescent- Alcohol 11% - Consumption Temperature between 10 and 11°C – Producer/Bottler Manuel N. F. de Faria.

DONATÁRIO – Type White – Year 1999 – Region Biscoitos – Colour Pale gold with green reflexes – Aroma Very fine of green fruit and a discreet smell of the sea (fresh seaweed)- Alcohol 12% - Consumption Temperature between 8 and 10°C – Producer/Bottler Casa Agrícola Brum Lda.

PEDRAS DO LOBO – Type White – Year 1997 – Region Biscoitos – Colour Gold pale emerald – Aroma Intense of tropical fruits with a touch of algae and a smell of the sea, and a slight touch of smoked wood - Alcohol 12,5% - Consump-

tion Temperature around 9°C – Producer/Bottler José Manuel de Sousa.

CHICO MARIA SECO – Type Liqueur-type – Year 1994 – Region Biscoitos – Colour Straw gold, with green tonalities – Aroma Elegant, of dried fruits (nuts, hazelnuts) highlighting certain spices - Alcohol 17% - Consumption Temperature around 8°C, as an aperitif or digestive – Producer/Bottler Casa Agrícola Brum Lda.

CHICO MARIA MEIO SECO – Tipo licoroso – Ano 1994 – Região Biscoitos – Cor ouro palha definido – Aroma fino, de tabaco e frutos secos – Álcool 18 % - Temperatura de consumo à volta de 10°C principalmente como aperitivo – Produtor/engarrafador Casa Agrícola Brum Lda.

CHICO MARIA DOCE – Type Liqueur-type – Year 1994 – Region Biscoitos – Colour Pale new gold – Aroma Algae, a smell of the sea, fine wood - Alcohol 19% - *Consopa* Temp. around 10°C, especially as an aperitif – Producer/Bottler Casa Agrícola Brum Lda" (*Vinhos dos Açores*, by Armando Mendes, DRDA edition).

"CURRALETA – Type Table wine – Year 1999 – Region Biscoitos – Colour Straw with green tonalities – Aroma Woodsy, intense of marine algae

- Alcohol 11,5% - Consumption Temperature between 8 and 10°C – Producer/Bottler Duarte Manuel Rocha Pires" (Bulletin by the Confraria do Vinho Verdelho dos Biscoitos Year VI n° 6 – 2001).

Others wines:

"Terra do Conde – white – Graciosa

Basalto – red – Pico

Curral Atlantis – red – Pico" (Vinhos dos Açores, by Armando Mendes, DRDA edition)

Also found in shopping areas are some liqueurs, which although not homemade, have already quite a few appreciators.

Cheese of the Azores

With the collaboration of many dairy cooperative societies, I will attempt to give you an idea of the cheeses we have in the Archipelago. From the start I apologise if, without meaning to, any are missing. And I will immediately begin with the smallest island – Corvo.

Queijo do Corvo – it is a cheese with an approximate weight of 1 kg and it is made of crude cow milk. It is subject to a sun-drying process of at least 60 days. Producer, Lacti-Corvo.

Queijo Uniflores – has an approximate weight of 8 kg and it is made of pasteurised cow milk. It is subject to a sun-drying process of at least 60 days. Producer, Cooperativa Agrícola das Flores.

Queijo Ilha Azul (Faial) – it is a plate-like cheese with an approximate weight of 600 g and it is made of pasteurised cow milk. It is subject to a sun-drying process of at least 30 days. Producer, C.A.L.F.

Queijo do Pico – D.O.P. – it is a soft paste-like cheese with an approximate weight of 600 g and it is made of crude cow milk.

Queijo de S. João, likewise from Pico, of equal weight and primary material, but without denomination. Producer, Queijaria do Pico.

Queijo de S. Jorge – island-type. Approximate weight of 9kg. Made of crude cow milk, with a sun-drying process of at least 120 days.

Queijo dos Lourais – island-type. Approximate weight of 9kg. Made of crude cow milk, with a sun-drying process of at least 90 days. Producer, of the two previous ones, C. A. dos Lourais..

Queijo do Topo – island-type. Approximate weight of 10kg, and it is made of crude cow milk. Sun-drying process, 90 days. Producer, Finisterra.

Graciosa – island-type cheese, with an approximate weight of 8 kg, made of crude cow milk. Sun-drying process, 90 days. Producer, União das Coop. da Graciosa.

From the island of Terceira, the following may be mentioned:

Castelinho – a cheese of soft texture with a semi-soft paste of a *sui generis* flavour with 30% of fat. Approximate weight, 1kg made with pasteurised milk, selected yeast, curdling and salt. Sun-drying process of at least 21 days. Producer, Unicol.

Ilha Branca – island-type cheese, approximate weight 8,5 to 9kg. Made with crude cow milk. Sup. fat at 45%. Sun-drying process of at least 3 months. Producer, União Coop. da Terceira G.V.M.S. (Coop A da Graciosa).

Queijo Bravo – a soft paste cheese, of mild flavour and aroma. Approximate weight of 1kg. Made of pasteurised cow milk. Producer, Soterlac.

Queijo Bravo Extra – a semi-soft paste cheese with a brownish crust. Made with the milk of cow, sheep and goat. Producer, Soterlac.

Queijo Bravo Tipo Ilha – a semi-hard paste cheese of yellowish colour. Weight between 7 and 8 kg. Made with pasteurised milk. Producer, Soterlac.

Queijo Vaquinha tradicional – cheese made with pasteurised cow milk. Is subject to a sun-drying process of 25 days.

Queijo Vaquinha "O Ilha Terceira" – cheese made with pasteurised cow milk. Is subject to a sun-drying process of 45 days. Normal size, 800 g.

Queijo Vaquinha picante – cheese made with pasteurised cow milk, adding malaguetta paste. Is subject to a sun-drying process of 45 days. Normal size, 800 g, although it may make cheeses of 10 kg, with a sun-drying process of 3 months, of the last two varieties. Producer of the 3 Vaquinha cheeses, João Henrique Melo Costa.

From the island of Terceira, the following may be mentioned:

Queijo Serra do Fogo – cheese of yellow paste, and mild flavour, soft and flexible. Weight, approximately, 900g. Shape: like a full plate. Producer, Lacto-Ibérica S.A.

Queijo Terra Nostra – cheese of the same producer, it is a cheese of light yellow paste, closed, soft, flexible. Approximate weight, 1,450kg. Shape: full ball.

Queijo Loreto – yellow paste cheese, closed, soft, flexible. Approximate weight, 1,450kg. Shape: full ball. Producer, also Lacto-Ibérica S.A.

Queijo Ilha "Famoso" – is subject to a sun-drying process of 1 month.

Queijo com alho e salsa – is subject to a sun-drying process of 1 month. Producer of these last 3, Unileite.

Final Remark – There is much more to recollect, with regards to so many other traditional specialities – the *massa sovada*, by the Holy Ghost, the *Filhoses de forno e fritas*, and the *Malaçadas*, around Carnival, the thick Papas on the 1st of May, the blood sausages or *morcelas* and the *linguiça* at the Parish feasts, the *Folares* around Easter and so many others.

MENUS SUGGESTIONS

MENU Nº 1
Fish Broth from Pico
Rice Rissoles

MENU Nº 2
Sour Soup
Torresmos in Garlic and Wine Sauce
1 small glass of a liqueur-type of wine

MENU Nº 3
Milk Bread Soup
Bran Pudding

MENU Nº 4
Fennel Soup
Green Tea Pudding

MENU Nº 5
Dried Mackerel with Raw Sauce
Broth of Turnips from the Land

MENU Nº 6
Rump
Clouded Eggs

MENU Nº 7
Grouper Pies
Dona Amélia
Milk Liqueur

MENU Nº 8
Clams
Roasted Meato of the *Manadas*
Espécies

MENU Nº 9
Limpet *Sarrabulho*
Molha à la mode de Pico
Cornucopias

MENU Nº 10
Stuffed Saurels
Soaked Li

MENU Nº 11
Octopus *à la mode de* Lages
Descaída

TABLE OF CONTENTS

AUTHOR: Zita Lima
RECIPE PREPARATION: Zita Lima
PHOTOGRAPHS: João Costa – Fotaçor
TRANSLATION: Marisa Roberto

THANKS BY THE AUTHOR:
I would like to express my thanks to my good
friends Guiomar Rosa, Professor Hélder Melo
and Vasco Pereira da Costa.
I would also like to thank the collaboration of:
ARMAZÉNS ZEFERINO – Angra do Heroísmo
SOTERLAC
CASA BRUM – Biscoitos
JOÃO HENRIQUE MELO COTA
ÂNGELO AMARAL

EDITORIAL MANAGEMENT:
Raquel López Varela
EDITORIAL COORDENATION:
Carla Rodrigues Pires
DESIGN CONCEPT OF THE COLLECTION:
Ricardo Barros – TTdesigncomunicação
LAYOUT:
Gráfica 99

© Zita Lima and
EVEREST EDITORA, LDA.
Pq. Ind. Meramar II, amz 1 and 2
2635-047 Rio de Mouro Portugal
ISBN: 989-50-0308-0
Legal Deposit: 235506/05
Printing Date: November.05
Printed in Spain
Editorial Evergráficas, S.L.
www.everest.pt